Blender
Drinks

Blender
Drinks

**Delicious fresh juices, smoothies, shakes
and whips to make in your blender**

Jan Purser, Dimitra Stais
and Tracy Rutherford

APPLE

Contents

The Blender Way

Fresh juices, smoothies, shakes, and whips are so quick to prepare and they provide the ideal boost needed for our fast and busy lifestyles. This book will show you how to make a range of drinks, all using a blender.

There is no limit to the variety that can be created as there is an amazing array of fresh fruit and vegetables available. The drinks in this book contain vitamins, minerals, live enzymes and other nutrients and, most importantly, they taste wonderful. We have divided this book into three sections: Energy Blends, guaranteed to provide you with a burst of energy with which to start your day; Refreshing Fruit Coolers that will cleanse and refresh you, perfect for any time; and Healthy Drinks, some using dairy-free alternatives, and all containing ingredients that will boost your vitamin levels and help improve your well-being.

If any of the drinks in this book seem a little stronger than you would like, you can dilute them with water. It is a good idea to dilute juices for children, as their digestive systems are more delicate than adults'.

There are many blenders available, and they vary in size and power. When choosing one, check how easy it is to clean and reassemble, and whether it has more than one speed. Also check the motor size – it is a good idea to select one that can handle ice cubes, which can overwork less powerful motors. Some blenders come with a handy grinder for coffee beans, nuts and seeds. Although blenders range in price, you should invest in a good-quality one that will last for years without problems.

We hope you enjoy our recipes as much as we've enjoyed developing and tasting them with our friends.

Happy blending!

Energy Blends

Smoothies, Shakes and Breakfast Pick-me-ups

Breakfast Smoothie

1 cup (8 fl oz/250 ml) milk or fortified soy milk, chilled
¼ cup (2 oz/60 g) plain (natural) acidophilus yogurt
4 oz (125 g) fresh strawberries, hulled, or thawed frozen strawberries
pulp of 2 passion fruits
2 teaspoons wheat germ
2 teaspoons honey or sugar

● In a blender, combine all the ingredients and process until smooth.
● Makes about 2½ cups (20 fl oz/625 ml); serves 2

Fig and Plum Shake

3 dried figs, chopped
3 dried dates, pitted, and chopped
¾ cup (6 fl oz/180 ml) water
2 red-fleshed plums, pitted, and chopped
1 cup (8 fl oz/250 ml) soy milk
1 tablespoon sunflower seed meal
1 tablespoon almond meal

● In a small saucepan, combine the figs, dates, and ¾ cup (6 fl oz/180 ml) water. Bring to a boil, then reduce heat, cover, and simmer until soft, about 10 minutes. Let cool. Transfer to a blender and add the plums, soy milk, and sunflower seed and almond meals. Blend until smooth and frothy. Thin with more water to taste before serving.
● Makes about 2½ cups (20 fl oz/625 ml); serves 2

Banana and Passionfruit Smoothie

2 small bananas, peeled, and chopped
2 cups (16 fl oz/500 ml) soy milk
4 teaspoons honey
2 teaspoons vanilla extract (essence)
pulp of 2 passion fruits

● In a blender, combine bananas, soy milk, honey and vanilla and blend until smooth. Stir in passion fruits and serve.
● Makes about 2¹/₂ cups (20 fl oz/625 ml); serves 2

Persimmon or Mango Shake

7 oz (210 g) peeled, pitted, and chopped persimmon or mango
1 cup (8 fl oz/250 ml) milk or fortified soy milk
¹/₂ cup (4 oz/125 g) plain (natural) acidophilus yogurt
pulp of 1 medium passion fruit
3 teaspoons wheat germ
3 teaspoons sunflower seed kernels
¹/₃ cup (3 fl oz/80 ml) water

● In a blender, combine all the ingredients and blend until smooth. Add a little extra water if necessary to reach a drinkable consistency.
● Makes about 3 cups (24 fl oz/750 ml); serves 3

Banana and Carob Shake

1 cup (8 fl oz/250 ml) low-fat milk or fortified soy milk
1 banana, peeled, and chopped
3 teaspoons carob powder
2 teaspoons oat bran
2 teaspoons almond meal or ground almonds

● In a blender, process the ingredients until smooth.
● Makes about 1¹/₂ cups (12 fl oz/375 ml); serves 1

Banana and Passionfruit Smoothie

Strawberry and Banana Breakfast Shake

1 cup (8 fl oz/250 ml) milk
1/2 cup (4 oz/125 g) plain (natural) acidophilus yogurt
1 ripe banana, peeled and chopped
4 oz/125 g fresh strawberries, hulled, or thawed frozen strawberries
2 tablespoons almond meal
1 tablespoon sunflower seed meal
2 teaspoons wheat germ

● In a blender, combine all the ingredients and process until smooth and frothy.
● Makes about 2 1/2 cups (20 fl oz/625 ml); serves 2

Strawberry Oat Milk Shake

1 cup (8 fl oz/250 ml) oat milk
4 oz/125 g fresh strawberries, hulled, or thawed frozen strawberries
1 tablespoon wheat germ
pinch ground cinnamon
1 teaspoon honey

● In a blender, combine all the ingredients and blend until smooth and frothy. Serve immediately.
● Makes about 1 1/2 cups (12 fl oz/375 ml); serves 1

Banana and Fig Smoothie

4 dried figs, chopped
1 cup (8 fl oz/250 ml) water
1 large banana, peeled, and chopped
1 cup (8 fl oz/250 ml) milk
1 tablespoon flaxseed (linseed) meal
1 tablespoon protein whey powder

● Put the figs in a small saucepan and add the water. Bring to a boil, then reduce heat, cover, and simmer until the figs are soft, about 10 minutes. In a blender, combine figs and their liquid and all the remaining ingredients. Process until smooth and frothy.
● Makes about 1 3/4 cups (14 fl oz/440 ml); serves 1–2

Strawberry and Banana Breakfast Shake

Yogurt Fruit Drink

4 cups (32 fl oz/1 L) soy milk
1 cup (8 fl oz/250 ml) plain (natural) acidophilus yogurt
2 tablespoons honey, or more as needed
choice of fruit: 4 kiwis (Chinese Gooseberries), peeled, and halved;
  1 cup (8 oz/250 g) hulled strawberries; 2 bananas, peeled, and
  sliced; 1 cups (4 oz/125 g) raspberries; 2 mangoes (about
  1¹/₂ lb/750 g), peeled, pitted, and cut in chunks

● Combine all ingredients in blender and add fruit of choice.
Process until smooth. Add more honey if desired.
● Makes about 6¹/₂ cups (52 fl oz/1625 ml); serves 4

Peach and Raisin Shake

¹/₃ cup (2 oz/60 g) golden raisins (sultanas)
2 peaches, peeled, pitted, and chopped
1 cup (8 fl oz/250 ml) soy milk
pinch ground cinnamon

● Put the raisins in a small bowl and add boiling water to cover.
Let stand for 5 minutes, then drain. In a blender, combine the
raisins and the remaining ingredients. Process until smooth and
frothy.
● Makes about 2 cups (8 fl oz/500 ml); serves 2

Banana and Peanut Butter Smoothie

1 cup (8 fl oz/250 ml) low-fat milk or fortified soy milk
1 large banana, peeled, and chopped
2 teaspoons carob powder
1 tablespoon peanut butter
2 teaspoons palm sugar

● In a blender, process all the ingredients until smooth.
● Makes about 1¹/₂ cups (12 fl oz/375 ml); serves 1

Banana and Apricot Thick Shake

10 dried apricots (about 2¹/₂ oz/75g)
1¹/₂ cups (12 fl oz/375 ml) milk or fortified soy milk, chilled
¹/₂ cup (4 oz/125 g) plain (natural) acidophilus yogurt or soy yogurt
1 medium banana, peeled, and chopped
2 teaspoons honey
4 ice cubes

● Put the apricots in a small bowl and add boiling water to cover. Let sit for 15 minutes. Drain and let cool to room temperature. In a blender, combine the apricots with all the remaining ingredients and process until smooth.
● Makes about 2³/₄ cups (22 fl oz/680 ml); serves 2–3

Passion Fruit and Banana Shake

pulp of 1 medium passion fruit
1 medium banana, peeled, and chopped
³/₄ cup (6 fl oz/180 ml) low-fat milk or fortified soy milk, chilled
¹/₄ cup (2 oz/60 g) vanilla yogurt

● In a blender, combine all the ingredients and blend until smooth.
● Makes about 1¹/₂ cups (12 fl oz/375 ml); serves 1

Chocolate Banana Shake

1 medium sugar/lady finger banana, peeled and chopped
³/₄ cup (6 fl oz/180 ml) low-fat milk or fortified soy milk
1 teaspoon unsweetened cocoa powder
1 teaspoon wheat germ

● In a blender, combine all the ingredients and blend until smooth.
● Makes about 1¹/₄ cups (10 fl oz/300 ml); serves 1

Tahini, Apricot and Peach Blend

1 large peach, peeled, pitted, and chopped
2 fresh figs, chopped
1 cup (8 fl oz/250 ml) apricot nectar
1 tablespoon tahini (sesame paste)
pinch ground cardamom
filtered or spring water to taste (optional)

● In a blender, combine all the ingredients except the water and process until smooth. Thin with a small amount of water to taste, if desired.
● Makes about 2 cups (16 fl oz/500 ml); serves 2

Carob and Strawberry Milkshake

1 cup (4 oz/125 g) fresh strawberries, hulled, or thawed frozen
    strawberries
3/4 cup (6 fl oz/180 ml) milk
1 tablespoon carob powder
1 tablespoon almond meal
1 1/2 teaspoons palm sugar

● In a blender, process all the ingredients until smooth and frothy.
● Makes about 1 1/2 cups (12 fl oz/375 ml); serves 1

Spiced Pistachio Smoothie

1/4 cup (1 oz/30 g) unsalted, shelled pistachios
1 cup (8 fl oz/250 ml) milk
1/2 cup (4 oz/125 g) vanilla yogurt
pinch ground cardamon
pinch ground cinnamon
1 teaspoon superfine (caster) sugar, or to taste
few drops rose water to taste, optional
6 ice cubes

● Place all ingredients in a blender and process until smooth and frothy.
● Makes about 2 cups (16 fl oz/500 ml); serves 2

Prune, Honey and Oat Milk Drink

6 prunes, pitted and chopped
3/4 cup (6 fl oz/180 ml) water
1 teaspoon honey
pinch saffron threads
1 tablespoon hot water
1 cup (8 fl oz/250 ml) oat milk
3/4 cup (6 oz/180 g) apricot acidophilus yogurt

● In a small saucepan, combine the prunes and water. Bring to a boil, then reduce heat, cover, and simmer until the prunes are soft, about 10 minutes. Let cool. In a small bowl, combine the honey and saffron. Add the hot water and stir to dissolve the honey. Let stand to soften the saffron, about 5 minutes. In a blender, combine the prunes and their liquid, the oat milk, yogurt, and saffron liquid. Process until smooth and frothy.
● Makes about 2 cups (16 fl oz/500 ml); serves 2

Banana and Almond Drink

1 large banana, peeled, and chopped
1 tablespoon almond meal
1 tablespoon tahini (sesame paste)
1 cup (8 fl oz/250 ml) low-fat milk
1/2 tablespoon carob powder
1 teaspoon honey (optional)

● In a blender, combine all the ingredients and process until smooth and frothy.
● Makes about 1 1/2 cups (12 fl oz/375 ml); serves 1

Pear and Mango Shake

3 oz (90 g) mango, peeled, pitted, and chopped
³/₄ cup (6 fl oz/180 ml) low-fat milk or fortified soy milk
1 teaspoon wheat germ
2 oz (60 g) natural acidophilus yogurt
4¹/₂ oz (140 g) canned pears in natural juice, drained
honey or sugar, to taste

- In a blender, combine all ingredients and blend until smooth.
- Makes about 1¹/₂ cups (12 fl oz/375 ml); serves 1

Pear and Date Shake

6 dried dates, pitted and chopped
³/₄ cup (6 fl oz/180 ml) water
1 teaspoon blackstrap molasses
2 pears, unpeeled, cored, and chopped
¹/₂ cup (4 fl oz/125 ml) rice milk

- In a small saucepan, combine the dates and water. Bring to a boil, then reduce heat, cover, and simmer until the dates are soft, about 10 minutes. Set aside to cool. In a small bowl, combine 1 tablespoon of the hot date liquid and the molasses; stir until dissolved. In a juicer, process the pears. In a blender, combine the dates and their juice, the dissolved molasses, and the rice milk. Process until smooth and frothy.
- Makes about 1 cup (8 fl oz/250 ml); serves 1

Chocolate Orange Shake

1¹/₂ cups (12fl oz/375 ml milk)
1 cup (8 oz/250 g) vanilla ice cream
1 tablespoon chocolate syrup
1 teaspoon finely grated orange zest

- Combine all ingredients in a blender and process briefly until frothy.
- Makes about 1¹/₂ cups (20 fl oz/625 ml); serves 1

Blackcurrant and Orange Egg-flip

3/4 cup (6 fl oz/180 ml) milk or fortified soy milk, chilled
3¹/2 oz (100 g) frozen black currants or other berries, thawed
1 egg
¹/4 cup (2 fl oz/60 ml) water
2 teaspoons honey, or to taste
1 teaspoon grated orange zest
¹/2 teaspoon brewer's yeast

● In a blender, combine all ingredients and blend until smooth.
● Makes about 1¹/4 cups (10 fl oz/300 ml): serves 1

Raisin and Cocoa Shake

2 oz (60 g) golden raisins (sultanas)
1 cup (8 fl oz/250 ml) milk or fortified soy milk, chilled
1 tablespoon unsweetened cocoa powder
1 teaspoon finely grated orange zest
1 teaspoon sugar

● Put the raisins in a small saucepan and add water to cover. Bring to a boil, then reduce heat to medium–low, cover and cook for 10 minutes. Drain and let cool to room temperature. In a blender, combine the raisins and all the remaining ingredients and blend until smooth.
● Makes about 1 cup (8 fl oz/250 ml); serves 1

Date and Plum Soy Shake

6 dates, pitted and chopped
¹/4 cup (2 fl oz/60 ml) water
2 canned dark plums in natural juice, drained, halved, and pitted
3/4 cup (6 fl oz/180 ml) hot soy milk

● In a small saucepan, combine the dates and the water. Bring to a boil, stirring until the mixture forms a paste. Spoon into a blender. Add the plums and soy milk and blend until smooth.
● Makes about 1¹/2 cups (12 fl oz/375 ml); serves 1

Blackcurrant and Orange Egg Flip

Fruit Lassi

1 cup (8 oz/250 g) natural yogurt
1 cup (8 fl oz/250 ml) milk
1¹/2 cups (12 oz/375 g) chopped fresh fruit (peach, mango or
  raspberry)
sugar to taste
crushed ice cubes
fresh fruit, leaves or flowers for garnish

⬤ In a blender, combine yogurt, milk, and 1 cup (8 oz/250 g) of
the chopped fruit. Process until frothy, about 20 seconds. Add
sugar. Fill glasses with crushed ice, pour in yogurt mixture and
top each with a portion of the remaining ¹/2 cup (4 oz/125 g) of
chopped fruit. Garnish with fruit, flowers or leaves.
⬤ Makes about 4 cups (32 fl oz/1 L); serves 4

Mango and Cumin Lassi

³/4 teaspoon cumin seeds
1¹/4 cups (10 oz/300 g) plain (natural) acidophilus yogurt
1¹/4 cups (10 fl oz/300 ml) non-fat milk
1 mango, peeled, pitted, and chopped
superfine (caster) sugar to taste
crushed ice for serving

⬤ Place cumin seeds in a nonstick pan over medium heat and
toast until aromatic, 1–2 minutes. Remove from pan and allow
to cool. Place ¹/2 teaspoon cumin seeds, yogurt, milk and mango
in a blender and process until thick. Sweeten to taste with sugar.
Place a handful of crushed ice into each glass. Pour lassi over ice.
Sprinkle lightly with remaining cumin seeds.
⬤ Makes about 4 cups (32 fl oz/1 L); serves 4

Refreshing Fruit Coolers
Fruity Whips, Cleansing Juices and Non-alcoholic Cocktails

Pineapple Lime Cooler

3 cups (24 fl oz/750 ml) pineapple juice
2 tablespoons lime juice
2 tablespoons superfine (caster) sugar, or more as needed
12 ice cubes
1 cup (8 fl oz/250 ml) club soda (soda water)
4 lime slices (optional)

● Place the pineapple juice, lime juice, sugar and ice cubes in a blender and process until the ice is crushed and the mixture is smooth. Taste for sugar and add more, 1 teaspoon at a time, if necessary. Pour into tall glasses until two-thirds full, top with club soda and serve immediately, garnished with lime slices if desired.
● Makes about 4 cups (32 fl oz/1 L); serves 4

Lime Lemonade

1/2 cup (4 fl oz/125 ml) lemon juice
1/2 cup (4 fl oz/125 ml) lime juice
1 cup (6 1/2 oz/200 g) superfine (caster) sugar
4 cups (32 fl oz/1 L) club soda (soda water)
8–10 mint leaves
ice cubes

● Combine the lemon juice, lime juice and sugar in a small saucepan over low heat and cook, stirring to dissolve sugar, for 3–4 minutes. Remove from heat and pour into a heatproof container. Refrigerate covered until completely cold, about 2 hours. To serve, add club soda and mint leaves and stir to combine. Place ice cubes in glasses and pour in over the lime lemonade.
● Makes about 4 cups (32 fl oz/1 L); serves 4

Berry and Orange Juice

1 cup (4 oz/125 g) fresh blueberries or thawed frozen blueberries
1 cup (4 oz/125 g) fresh cranberries or thawed frozen cranberries
1 cup (4 oz/125 g) fresh strawberries, hulled, or thawed frozen
  strawberries
1/2-inch (12-mm) piece fresh ginger, finely grated
2 teaspoons finely grated orange zest

● In a blender, process the berries and grated ginger. Whisk in
the orange zest. Thin with a little water, if desired.
● Makes about ¾ cup (6 fl oz/180 ml); serves 1

Plum and Berry Blend

1 cup (4 oz/125 g) fresh loganberries or blackberries or thawed frozen
  loganberries or blackberries
1 cup (4 oz/125 g) fresh strawberries, hulled, or thawed frozen
  strawberries
3 large red-fleshed plums, pitted, and chopped

● Place all the ingredients in a blender, and process until
smooth. Thin with a little water if desired.
● Makes about 1 cup (8 fl oz/250 ml); serves 1

Blackberry Juice

4 oz (125 g) blackberries or pitted cherries
1 medium pear, peeled, cored, and chopped
3 teaspoons oat bran

● Blend the blackberries and pear in a blender. Thin with a little
water, if desired. Whisk in the oat bran.
● Makes about 1 cup (8 fl oz/250 ml); serves 1

Mango Frappe

1 mango, peeled, pitted, and chopped
1/4 pineapple, peeled, cored, and chopped
1/4 papaya, peeled, seeded, and chopped
1/2 lime, peeled, seeded, and chopped

● Place all ingredients in a blender, and process until smooth.
● Makes about 2 cups (16 fl oz/500 ml); serves 2

Orange, Pineapple and Mango Juice

1 large orange, peeled, seeded, and chopped
1 mango, peeled, pitted, and chopped
1/4 pineapple, peeled, cored, and chopped

● Place all ingredients in a blender, and process until smooth.
● Makes about 1 1/4 cups (10 fl oz/300 ml); serves 1

Peppermint and Mango Drink

1 peppermint tea bag
3/4 cup (6 fl oz/180 ml) boiling water
1 large fresh mango, peeled, pitted, and chopped,
*   or 6 oz (180 g) frozen mango flesh*
1 teaspoon acidophilus powder

● Put the tea bag in a cup and add the boiling water. Cover and
let steep for 10 minutes. Remove the tea bag and let the tea cool.
In a blender, combine the tea, mango and acidophilus powder
and process until smooth.
● Makes about 1 1/4 cups (10 fl oz/300 ml); serves 1

Mango Frappe

Prune and Apple Smoothie

2 oz (60 g) pitted prunes
1 cup (8 fl oz/250 ml) water
good pinch black pepper
1/2 cup (4 fl oz/125 ml) apple juice

In a saucepan, combine the prunes and water. Bring to a boil, then reduce heat, cover, and simmer for 10 minutes. Set aside to cool. In a blender, combine prunes and their liquid with remaining ingredients and blend until smooth.

Makes about 3/4 cup (6 fl oz/180 ml); serves 1

Kiwi, Apple and Grape Juice

1 kiwifruit, peeled and chopped
1/2 cup (4 fl oz/125 ml) apple juice
7 oz (220 g) seedless red grapes, chopped

In a blender, combine all the ingredients and process until smooth.

Makes about 1 1/4 cups (10 fl oz/300 ml); serves 1

Apple and Citrus Juice

1 ginseng tea bag or sachet
1/2 cup (4 fl oz/125 ml) boiling water
1 large orange, peeled, seeded, and chopped
1 small lime, peeled, seeded, and chopped
1 apple, peeled, cored, and grated

Put the ginseng tea bag in a cup and add the boiling water. Let steep for 10 minutes, then remove the tea bag and refrigerate the tea until cold, about 20 minutes. In a blender, process the orange, lime, and apple. Pour in the tea and stir to combine.

Makes about 1 1/4 cups (10 fl oz/300 ml); serves 1

Kiwi and Cantaloupe Juice

¹/₄ cantaloupe (rockmelon), peeled, seeded, and chopped
2 kiwifruit, peeled and chopped
8 ice cubes

● Place all the ingredients in a blender and process until smooth.
● Makes about 2 cups (16 fl oz/500 ml); serves 2

Peach, Plum and Raspberry Juice

1 peach, peeled, pitted, and chopped
2 red-fleshed plums, pitted, and chopped
1 cup (4 oz/125 g) fresh raspberries or thawed frozen raspberries

● Place all the ingredients in a blender and process until smooth.
● Makes about 1¹/₂ cups (12 fl oz/375 ml); serves 1

Passionfruit and Berry Frappe

pulp of 2 passion fruits
¹/₄ pineapple, peeled, cored, and chopped
¹/₂ cup (2 oz/60g) fresh blueberries or thawed frozen blueberries
8 ice cubes

● Place all the ingredients in a blender and process until smooth.
● Makes about 2 cups (16 fl oz/500 ml); serves 2

Apricot and Brazil Blend

¹/₄ cup (1¹/₂ oz/45 g) dried apricots
1 cup (8 fl oz/250 ml) water, plus filtered or spring cold water to taste
juice of 2 large oranges
6 Brazil nuts
1 tablespoon wheat germ

● In a small saucepan, combine the dried apricots and water. Bring to a boil, then reduce heat, cover, and simmer for 10 minutes. Set aside to cool. In a blender, combine the apricots and their liquid, and all remaining ingredients except the cold water, and process until smooth. Thin with cold water to desired consistency.
● Makes about 1¹/₄ cups (10 fl oz/300 ml); serves 1

Orange and Apricot Whip

4¹/₂ oz (140 g) canned apricots in natural juice
³/₄ cup (6 fl oz/180 ml) fresh orange juice
1 teaspoon grated fresh ginger
¹/₂ teaspoon wheat germ oil

● Place all the ingredients in a blender and process until smooth.
● Makes about 1¹/₃ cups (11 fl oz/330 ml); serves 1

Apricot and Cherimoya Whip

7 oz (220 g) cherimoya (custard apple), seeded
4¹/₂ oz (140 g) canned apricots in   juice
¹/₂ cup (4 fl oz/125 ml) fresh orange juice
3 teaspoons fresh lime juice

● Scoop the cherimoya flesh into a blender and discard skin. Add the remaining ingredients and process until smooth.
● Makes about 1¹/₄ cups (10 fl oz/300 ml); serves 1

Pineapple and Coconut Drink

1/2 pineapple, peeled, cored, and chopped
1/2 cup (4 fl oz/125 ml) coconut milk
6 fresh mint leaves, finely chopped

⬤ Place all the ingredients in a blender and process until smooth.
⬤ Makes about 1 1/2 cups (12 fl oz/375 ml); serves 1

Guava and Pineapple Drink

1/4 pineapple, peeled, cored, and chopped
1 large guava, cut into thin wedges

⬤ Place the ingredients in a blender and process until smooth.
⬤ Makes about 1 1/2 cups (12 fl oz/375 ml); serves 1

Pineapple, Cranberry and Orange Drink

1 orange, peeled, seeded, and chopped
1/4 pineapple, peeled, cored, and chopped
1 cup (8 fl oz/250 ml) cranberry juice
8 ice cubes

⬤ Combine all ingredients in a blender and process until smooth. Serve immediately.
⬤ Makes about 2 cups (16 fl oz/500 ml); serves 2

Mango and Banana Mix

1/2 mango, peeled, pitted, and chopped
1 banana, peeled and chopped
3/4 cup (6 fl oz/180 ml) apple juice
1 tablespoon pumpkin seed kernels (pepitas)

● Place all the ingredients in a blender and process until smooth. Add more apple juice if the drink appears too thick.
● Makes about 1 1/2 cups (12 fl oz/375 ml); serves 1

Papaya, Pineapple and Mango Frappe

1/4 papaya, peeled, seeded, and chopped
1/4 pineapple, peeled, cored, and chopped
1 mango, peeled, pitted, and chopped
4 basil leaves (optional)
8 cubes of ice

● Combine all ingredients in a blender and process until smooth.
● Makes about 2 cups (16 fl oz/500 ml); serves 2

Pear and Raspberry Juice

1 cup (4 oz/125 g) fresh raspberries or thawed frozen raspberries
1/2 pear, peeled, cored, and chopped
1/3 cup (3 fl oz/80 ml) water

● In a blender, combine all ingredients and process until smooth.
● Makes about 1 cup (8 fl oz/250 ml); serves 1

Peach and Raspberry Cocktail

2 ripe, juicy peaches, peeled, pitted, and chopped
1 cup (4 oz/125 g) fresh raspberries or thawed frozen raspberries
sparkling mineral water to taste

In a blender, puree the peaches and raspberries until smooth. Press through a fine-mesh sieve to remove the raspberry seeds. Pour into 2 tall glasses, then gradually add the mineral water to your preferred consistency. Stir gently to combine.

Makes about 1³/₄ cups (14 fl oz/440 ml); serves 2

Melon Berry Crush

1¹/₂ cups (8 oz/250 g) chopped and seeded watermelon flesh
¹/₄ cantaloupe (rockmelon), peeled, seeded, and chopped
1 cup (4 oz/125 g) fresh strawberries, hulled, or thawed frozen
  strawberries
ice cubes

In a blender, combine all the fruits and process until smooth. Serve immediately over ice.

Makes about 2 cups (16 fl oz/500 ml); serves 2

Tropicana

1 cup ice cubes
4 fl oz/120 ml pineapple juice
1 tablespoon lychee juice
¹/₄ cup pawpaw, peeled, seeded, and chopped
¹/₂ cup mango, peeled, pitted, and chopped
2 mint leaves

Place ice, juices, pawpaw and mango into a blender. Process and pour into a large cocktail or martini glass. Garnish with mint leaves.

Makes about 1 cup (8 fl oz/250 ml); serves 1

Tropical Colada

1 mango, peeled, pitted, and chopped
1/4 pineapple, peeled, cored, and chopped
ice cubes
1/2 cup (4 fl oz/125 ml) coconut milk

In a blender, process the mango and pineapple. Put a few ice cubes into 2 tall glasses and pour the juice over. Add half the coconut milk to each glass and stir to combine.

Makes about 1 3/4 cups (14 fl oz/440 ml); serves 2

Papaya and Pineapple Juice

1/2 small papaya, peeled, seeded, and chopped
1/2 small pineapple, peeled, cored, and chopped
1 large apple, peeled, cored, and grated
1/2 lemon, peeled, seeded, and chopped

In a blender, process all the ingredients until smooth. Thin with a little water, if desired.

Makes about 2 cups (16 fl oz/500 ml); serves 2

Strawberry and Pineapple Whip

4 oz (125 g) fresh strawberries, hulled, or thawed frozen strawberries
1/2 medium pear, peeled, cored, and chopped
1/4 medium pineapple, peeled, cored and chopped
1 orange, peeled, and chopped

In a blender, process all the ingredients until smooth and frothy.

Makes about 2 cups (16 fl oz/500 ml); serves 2

Banana and Mango Whip

1 banana, peeled, and chopped
1 small mango, peeled, pitted, and chopped
6 ice cubes

● In a blender, combine all the ingredients and process until smooth and frothy.
● Makes about 1 1/2 cups (12 fl oz/375 ml); serves 1

Tutti Frutti

6 strawberries, hulled
1/2 cup ice cubes
1 tablespoon apricot juice
1 tablespoon pineapple juice
1 tablespoon red ruby red grapefruit juice
1 tablespoon cranberry juice
1 tablespoon orange juice
1 tablespoon lemon juice
1/2 mango, peeled, pitted, and chopped
wedge of ruby red grapefruit

● Place strawberries into a blender and process. Pour into a glass. Rinse blender then add remaining ingredients. Process until smooth and pour over strawberry puree. Garnish with a wedge of grapefruit.
● Makes about 1 cup (8 fl oz/250 ml); serves 1

Watermelon Juice

2 1/2-lb (1.25-kg) piece watermelon, chilled, seeded, and chopped

● Process the watermelon in a blender.
● Makes about 2 cups (16 fl oz/500 ml); serves 2

Banana and Mango Whip

Healthy Drinks
Vitamin Boosters, Herbal Vitalizers, Low-fat and Soy Blends

Orange Anti-oxidant Juice

1 orange, peeled, seeded, and chopped
1/2 mango, peeled, pitted, and chopped
1/2 small papaya, peeled, seeded, and chopped
1/4 pineapple, peeled, cored, and chopped

● In a blender, process all the ingredients until smooth.
● Makes about 2 cups (16 fl oz/500 ml); serves 2

Vitamin C Juice

1 grapefruit, peeled, seeded, and chopped
1 large orange, peeled, seeded, and chopped
1 kiwifruit, peeled, and chopped

● In a blender, process all the ingredients until smooth.
● Makes about 1 cup (8 fl oz/250 ml); serves 1

Orange and Apricot Juice

5 dried apricots, finely chopped
1/2 cup (4 fl oz/125 ml) water
3/4 cup (6 fl oz/180 ml) fresh orange juice
1/2 oz (15 g) finely chopped fresh parsley

● In a saucepan, combine the apricots and water. Bring to a boil, then reduce heat, cover, and simmer for 15 minutes. Set aside to cool. In a blender, combine apricots and liquid and all remaining ingredients. Process until smooth.
● Makes about 1 cup (8 fl oz/250 ml); serves 1

Blueberry, Apricot and Hazelnut Shake

5 dried apricots, chopped
2 tablespoons hot water
1 cup (8 fl oz/250 ml) low-fat milk or fortified soy milk
8 hazelnuts
4 oz (125 g) fresh blueberries or thawed frozen blueberries

● Put the dried apricots in a small bowl and add the hot water. Let soak for 15 minutes, or until soft. In a blender, combine the apricots and their liquid with all the remaining ingredients and process until smooth.
● Makes about 1 1/3 cups (11 fl oz/330 ml); serves 1

Orange and Blueberry Drink

finely grated zest and juice of 1 1/2 large oranges
7 oz (220 g) fresh blueberries or thawed frozen blueberries

● In a blender, combine all the ingredients and blend until smooth.
● Makes about 1 1/4 cups (11 fl oz/340 ml); serves 1

Blueberry, Orange and Cantaloupe Juice

1/4 medium (12 oz/375 g) cantaloupe (rockmelon), peeled, seeded and chopped
1 large orange, peeled, seeded, and chopped
7 oz (250 g) fresh blueberries or thawed frozen blueberries

● Process ingredients in a blender. Mix well, adding a little water to thin, if desired.
● Makes about 1 1/4 cups (10 fl oz/330 ml); serves 1

Cherry Juice

14 oz (440 g) pitted fresh cherries or canned cherries, drained
¹/₂ cup (4 fl oz/125 ml) water

● In a blender, combine cherries and water and process until smooth.
● Makes about 1¹/₄ cups (10 fl oz/300 ml); serves 1

Cranberry and Apple Juice

2¹/₂ oz (75 g) fresh cranberries or thawed frozen cranberries
²/₃ cup (5 fl oz/150 ml) apple juice

● In a blender, combine cranberries and apple juice and process until smooth. Strain into a serving glass.
● Makes about ³/₄ cup (6 fl oz/180 ml); serves 1

Prune and Apple Drink

4 pitted prunes
³/₄ cup (6 fl oz/180 ml) water
2 apples, peeled, cored, and grated
1 cup (4 oz/125 g) fresh black currants or blueberries or thawed frozen
  black currants or blueberries

● Place the prunes and water in a small saucepan. Bring to a boil, then reduce heat, cover, and simmer for 10 minutes. Set aside to cool. Place all the ingredients in a blender and process until smooth.
● Makes about 1 cup (8 fl oz/250 ml); serves 1

Papaya and Mint Drink

6¹/₂ oz (200 g) papaya, peeled, seeded, and chopped
2 tablespoons plain (natural) acidophilus yogurt
1 teaspoon chopped fresh mint
¹/₂ cup (4 fl oz/125 ml) water

● In a blender, combine all ingredients and process until smooth.
● Makes about 1 cup (8 fl oz/250 ml); serves 1

Nectarine, Pineapple and Ginseng Drink

1 ginseng tea bag or sachet
¹/₂ cup (4 fl oz/125 ml) boiling water
¹/₄ pineapple, peeled, cored, and chopped
1 nectarine, pitted, and chopped

● Put the ginseng tea bag in a cup and add the boiling water. Let steep for 10 minutes, then remove the tea bag and refrigerate the tea until chilled, about 30 minutes. In a blender, process the pineapple, nectarine and tea until smooth.
● Makes about 1¹/₂ cups (12 fl oz/375 ml); serves 1

Pear, Licorice and Orange Drink

2 teaspoons dried licorice root, chopped
¹/₄ cup (2 fl oz/60 ml) boiling water
1 large pear, peeled, cored, and chopped
1 teaspoon finely grated orange zest

● In a small bowl, combine the licorice and boiling water. Cover and let steep for 10 minutes. Strain, reserving the liquid. In a blender, process the pear, licorice tea and orange zest until smooth.
● Makes about 1 cup (8 fl oz/250 ml); serves 1

Pineapple and Ginger Lifter

3/4-inch (2-cm) piece fresh ginger, finely grated
1/2 medium pineapple, peeled, cored, and chopped
1/2 teaspoon finely chopped fresh mint

● In a blender, process the ginger and pineapple until smooth. Stir in the mint.
● Makes about 1 cup (8 fl oz/250 ml); serves 1

Orange and Ginger Juice

2 oranges, peeled, seeded, and chopped
1/4 cantaloupe (rockmelon), peeled, seeded, and chopped
1/2-inch (12-mm) piece fresh ginger, finely grated

● In a blender, process all the ingredients until smooth.
● Makes about 13/4 cups (14 fl oz/440 ml); serves 1–2

Peach and Ginger Thick Shake

2 large peaches, peeled, pitted, and chopped
1/2 cup (4 oz/125 g) low-fat plain (natural) acidophilus yogurt
  or soy yogurt
1 cup (8 fl oz/250 ml) low-fat milk or fortified soy milk, chilled
2 teaspoons honey
pinch ground ginger

● In a blender, combine all the ingredients and process until smooth and frothy.
● Makes about 2 cups (16 fl oz/500 ml); serves 2

Orange and Sage Juice

2 oranges, peeled, and chopped
1 teaspoon finely chopped fresh sage
1 teaspoon grated orange zest
1/2 teaspoon wheat germ oil

● Process the orange in a blender. Whisk in the remaining ingredients.
● Makes about 1 cup (8 fl oz/250 ml); serves 1

Prune and Chamomile Drink

1 chamomile tea bag, or 1 teaspoon dried chamomile
3/4 cup (6 fl oz/180 ml) boiling water
1/2 cup (4 oz/125 g) plain (natural) acidophilus yogurt
6 prunes, pitted
1 teaspoon grated orange zest
1 teaspoon honey

● Put the tea bag or chamomile in a cup and add the boiling water. Let steep for 10 minutes. Strain, reserving the liquid. Chill the liquid. In a blender, combine the tea and all the remaining ingredients and process until smooth.
● Makes about 1 1/3 cups (11 fl oz/330 ml); serves 1

Chamomile Mango Strawberry Juice

1 chamomile tea bag
1/4 cup (2 fl oz/60 ml) boiling water
1/2 cup (4 fl oz/125 ml) low-fat milk or fortified soy milk, chilled
3 oz (90 g) mango, peeled, pitted, and chopped
4 oz (125 g) fresh strawberries, hulled, or thawed frozen strawberries
2 teaspoons wheat germ

● Put the chamomile tea bag in a cup and add the boiling water. Cover and let steep for 10 minutes. Remove the tea bag and let the tea cool. In a blender, combine the tea and all the remaining ingredients and process until smooth.
● Makes about 1 1/2 cups (12 fl oz/375 ml); serves 1

Cantaloupe, Blueberry and Mint Juice

1/2 cup (1/2 oz/15 g) finely chopped fresh parsley
10 fresh mint leaves
1/2 cantaloupe (rockmelon), peeled, seeded, and chopped
1 cup (4 oz/125 g) fresh, or thawed frozen, blueberries

- In a blender process all the ingredients until smooth.
- Makes about 1 1/2 cups (12 fl oz/375 ml); serves 1

Fennel and Apricot Shake

1 fennel tea bag
1/4 cup (2 fl oz/60 ml) boiling water
3/4 cup (6 fl oz/180 ml) milk or fortified soy milk
5 drained canned apricot halves
2 teaspoons ground almonds
1 teaspoon honey

- Put the tea bag in a cup and add boiling water. Leave to steep 15 minutes. Remove the tea bag and chill tea. In a blender, combine the tea and all the remaining ingredients and process until smooth.
- Makes about 1 3/4 cups (14 fl oz/440 ml); serves 2

Apricot, Orange and Ginger Smoothie

5 dried apricots, chopped
3/4 cup (6 fl oz/180 ml) water
juice of 1 large orange
2 teaspoons oat bran
1 teaspoon finely grated fresh ginger

- In saucepan, combine apricots and water. Bring to a boil, then reduce heat, cover, and simmer for 15 minutes. Set aside to cool. In a blender, combine the liquid and remaining ingredients and process until smooth.
- Makes about 1 1/4 cups (10 fl oz/300 ml); serves 1

Warm Grapefruit Drink

1 grapefruit or lemon
1/2 cup (4 fl oz/125 ml) hot water

● Squeeze the juice from the grapefruit using a citrus juicer, or peel and chop the grapefruit into small pieces and process in a blender. Pour into a cup and whisk in the hot water. Drink while warm.
● Makes about 1 1/4 cups (10 fl oz/300 ml) grapefruit drink, or 3/4 cup (6 fl oz/180 ml) lemon drink; serves 1

Peach and Honey Soother

1 chamomile tea bag
1/4 cup (2 fl oz/60 ml) boiling water
4 1/2 oz (140 g) canned peaches in natural juice, drained
1/2 cup (4 fl oz/125 ml) low-fat milk, warmed
1 teaspoon honey, or to taste

● Put the tea bag in a cup and add the water. Leave to steep for 10 minutes. Remove the tea bag and pour the liquid into a blender. Add the remaining ingredients and process until smooth.
● Makes about 1 1/4 cups (10 fl oz/300 ml); serves 1

Warm Apricot Smoothie

1/3 cup (2 oz/60 g) dried apricots
1 cup (8 fl oz/250 ml) water
3/4 cup (6 fl oz/185 ml) milk
pinch ground ginger
1 teaspoon honey, or to taste

● In a small saucepan, combine the dried apricots and water. Bring to a boil, then reduce heat, cover, and simmer for 10 minutes. Set aside to cool slightly. In a small saucepan, heat the milk until bubbles form around the edge of the pan. In a blender, combine the apricots and their liquid, the hot milk, ginger, and honey. Process until smooth. Drink warm.
● Makes about 1 1/4 cups (10 fl oz/300 ml); serves 1

Lime and Strawberry Soda

4 oz (125 g) fresh strawberries, hulled, or thawed frozen strawberries
1/2 lime, chopped
1/2 cup (4 fl oz/125 ml) soda water

● In a blender, process the strawberries, then the lime. Add the soda water and stir to combine.
● Makes about 1 cup (8 fl oz/250 ml); serves 1

Peach and Mango Low-fat Shake

3/4 cup (6 fl oz/180 ml) low-fat milk or low-fat fortified
   soy milk, chilled
41/2 oz (140 g) canned mixed peach and mango in natural
juice, chilled

● In a blender, combine all the ingredients and process until smooth.
● Makes about 11/4 cups (10 fl oz/300 ml); serves 1

Silky Mango Whip

1 tablespoon dried red clover
1/4 cup (2 fl oz/60 ml) boiling water
1 tablespoon flaxseed (linseed) meal
1/2 cup (5 oz/150 g) silken tofu
1 medium mango, peeled, pitted, and chopped,
   or 110 g frozen or canned mango
1/2 cup (4 fl oz/125 ml) apple juice

● In a cup, combine the red clover and boiling water. Leave to steep for 15 minutes. Strain, reserving the liquid. Place the red clover tea and all the remaining ingredients in a blender and process until smooth.
● Makes about 11/4 cups (10 fl oz/300 ml); serves 1

Apricot and Raspberry Smoothie

50 g dried apricots, chopped
¹/₂ cup (4 fl oz/125 ml) water
¹/₂ cup (4 fl oz/125 ml) low-fat milk or fortified soy milk
1 tablespoon tahini (sesame paste)
2¹/₂ oz/75 g fresh raspberries or thawed frozen raspberries
1 teaspoon honey, or to taste

● In a small saucepan, combine the apricots and water. Bring to a boil, then reduce heat, cover, and cook for 15 minutes. Set aside to cool. In a blender, combine apricots and liquid with remaining ingredients and process.
● Makes about 1¹/₂ cups (12 fl oz/375 ml); serves 1

Low-fat Banana Smoothie

4 cups (32 fl oz/1 L) non-fat milk
1 cup (8 fl oz/250 ml) low-fat plain (natural) acidophilus yogurt
2 bananas, peeled and sliced

● Combine all ingredients in a blender and process until smooth.
● Makes about 4 cups (32 fl oz/1 L); serves 4

Apple, Apricot and Almond Shake

5 dried apples
7 dried apricots
1 cup (8 fl oz/250 ml) boiling water
1¹/₄ cups (10 fl oz/300 ml) milk or fortified soy milk
¹/₄ cup (2 fl oz/60 ml) ice-cold water
1 oz (30 g) unblanched almonds
¹/₂ teaspoon vanilla extract (essence)

● Put apples and apricots in a bowl and add boiling water. Set aside to soak for 20 minutes. Drain fruit and cool. In a blender, combine drained fruit and remaining ingredients and process until smooth.
● Makes about 2¹/₂ cups (20 fl oz/625 ml); serves 2

Pink Plum Shake

3 small dark plums, halved and pitted
1 cup (8 fl oz (250 ml) milk or soy milk
1 egg
1 teaspoon wheat germ

● In a blender, combine all the ingredients and process until smooth.
● Makes about 1½ cups (12 fl oz/375 ml); serves 1

Nutty Apple Egg-flip

5 dried apples
¼ cup (2 fl oz/60 ml) hot water
1 cup (8 fl oz/250 ml) milk or fortified soy milk
4 Brazil nuts
1 egg
2 teaspoons wheat germ
¼ teaspoon vanilla extract (essence)

● In a small bowl, soak the apple in hot water for 15 minutes or until soft. In a blender, combine apple and liquid and remaining ingredients and process until smooth.
● Makes about 1¼ cups (10 fl oz/300 ml); serves 1

Tofu Thick Shake

1 cup (8 fl oz/250 ml) low-fat, calcium-enriched soy milk
¼ cup (2½ oz/75 g) silken tofu
1 tablespoon unsweetened cocoa powder
2 teaspoons honey
pinch ground cinnamon

● In a blender, combine all the ingredients and process until smooth and frothy.
● Makes about 1½ cups (12 fl oz/375 ml); serves 1

Berry Soy Smoothie

2 cups (8 oz/250 g) fresh strawberries, hulled, and/or raspberries
6$\frac{1}{2}$ oz (200 g) berry soy yogurt
$\frac{1}{2}$ cup (4 fl oz/125 ml) soy milk
2 teaspoons honey

- In a blender, process all ingredients until smooth.
- Variation: Substitute or add fresh or thawed frozen blueberries.
- Makes 2 cups (16 fl oz/500 ml); serves 2

Honeyed Strawberry Shake

6$\frac{1}{2}$ oz (200 g) silken tofu, drained
2 cups (8 oz/250 g) fresh strawberries, hulled
2 medium bananas, peeled and chopped
1$\frac{1}{2}$ cups (12 fl oz/375 ml) soy milk
2 teaspoons honey

- In a blender, combine tofu, strawberries and banana and puree for 2 minutes. Add soy milk and honey and continue processing until smooth.
- Makes about 2$\frac{1}{2}$ cups (20 fl oz/625 ml); serves 2

Cantaloupe and Pineapple Smoothie

1$\frac{1}{3}$ cups (8 oz/250 g) chopped cantaloupe (rockmelon)
$\frac{1}{2}$ cup (3 oz/90 g) fresh pineapple, peeled, cored, and chopped
1 cup (8 fl oz/250 ml) low-fat soy milk
1 tablespoon maple syrup
1 teaspoon chopped fresh mint or mint sprigs for garnish

- In a blender, combine cantaloupe and pineapple. Process for 2 minutes. Add soy milk and maple syrup and continue processing until smooth. Serve, garnished with mint.
- Makes 2$\frac{1}{2}$ cups (20 fl oz/625 ml); serves 2

Mango and Strawberry Soy Shake

¹/₂ mango, peeled, pitted, and chopped
4 oz (125 g) fresh strawberries, hulled, or thawed frozen strawberries
1 scoop (about 1 oz/30 g) low-fat ice cream
1 cup (8 fl oz/250 ml) milk or fortified soy milk

● In a blender, combine all the ingredients and process until smooth.
● Makes about 2 cups (16 fl oz/500 ml); serves 2

Strawberry and Pumpkin Seed Shake

¹/₂ cup (4 fl oz/125 ml) low-fat milk or fortified soy milk, chilled
4 oz (125 g) fresh strawberries, hulled, or thawed frozen strawberries
1 tablespoon pumpkin seed kernels (pepitas), ground
  or very finely chopped
2 teaspoons honey
¹/₄–¹/₂ teaspoon brewer's yeast, to taste

● In a blender, combine all the ingredients and process until smooth.
● Makes about 1 cup (8 fl oz/250 ml); serves 1

Fruity Soy Iceblocks

1 cup (7¹/₂ oz/235 g) pureed fruit such as, pineapple, peaches,
  strawberries, or bananas
¹/₂ cup (4 fl oz/125 ml) soy milk
1 tablespoon honey or maple syrup

● In a blender, combine all the ingredients, processing until smooth. Freeze in iceblock moulds for at least 2 hours, inserting wooden sticks after mixture has partially frozen.
● Variation: For extra creaminess, add ¹/₄ cup (2 oz/60 g) plain (natural) or flavoured soy yogurt to mixture.
● Makes about 6 iceblocks

Index

Weights and Measures

WEIGHTS	
Imperial	Metric
$1/3$ oz	10 g
$1/2$ oz	15 g
$3/4$ oz	20 g
1 oz	30 g
2 oz	60 g
3 oz	90 g
4 oz ($1/4$ lb)	125 g
5 oz ($1/3$ lb)	150 g
6 oz	180 g
7 oz	220 g
8 oz ($1/2$ lb)	250 g
9 oz	280 g
10 oz	300 g
11 oz	330 g
12 oz ($3/4$ lb)	375 g
16 oz (1 lb)	500 g
2 lb	1 kg
3 lb	1.5 kg
4 lb	2 kg
5 lb	2.5 kg

VOLUME		
Imperial	Metric	Cup
1 fl oz	30 ml	
2 fl oz	60 ml	$1/4$
3	90 ml	$1/3$
4	125 ml	$1/2$
5	150 ml	$2/3$
6	180 ml	$3/4$
8	250 ml	1
10	300 ml	$1 1/4$
12	375 ml	$1 1/2$
13	400 ml	$1 2/3$
14	440 ml	$1 3/4$
16	500 ml	2
24	750 ml	3
32	1L	4

USEFUL CONVERSIONS	
$1/4$ teaspoon	1.25 ml
$1/2$ teaspoon	2.5 ml
1 teaspoon	5 ml
1 Australian tablespoon	20 ml (4 teaspoons)
1 UK/US tablespoon	15 ml (3 teaspoons)

A LANSDOWNE BOOK

Published by Apple Press
Sheridan House
4th Floor
112–116A Western Road
Hove
East Sussex BN3 1DD UK

ISBN 1 84092 384 9

This book was designed and produced by Lansdowne Publishing Pty Ltd
Sydney NSW 2000, Australia

Designer: Avril Makula
Production Manager: Sally Stokes
Project Co-ordinator: Kathleen Davidson

Set in Giovanni Book on Quark XPress
Printed in Singapore by Imago

To Sam, Daniel, Jack, Adam, Ella and Lydia

S.McB.

To Di, Steve, Deirdre and The Mice

A.J.

First published 2007 as a slipcase edition containing four individual stories
by Walker Books Limited, 87 Vauxhall Walk, London SE11 5HJ
This edition published 2009
2 4 6 8 10 9 7 5 3 1

Text © 2007 Sam McBratney
Illustrations © 2007 Anita Jeram

Guess How Much I Love You™ is a registered
trademark of Walker Books Ltd, London

The right of Sam McBratney and Anita Jeram to be
identified as author and illustrator respectively of this
work has been asserted by them in accordance with
the Copyright, Designs and Patents Act 1988

This book has been typeset in Cochin

Printed and bound in China

British Library Cataloguing in
Publication Data: a catalogue record
for this book is available from the
British Library

ISBN 978-1-4063-1604-9

www.walker.co.uk

GUESS HOW MUCH I LOVE YOU

All Year Round

Written by
Sam McBratney

Illustrated by
Anita Jeram

WALKER BOOKS
AND SUBSIDIARIES
LONDON · BOSTON · SYDNEY · AUCKLAND

Spring

Little Nutbrown Hare
and Big Nutbrown Hare went
hopping in the spring.

Spring is when things start
growing after winter.

They saw a tiny acorn growing.

"Someday it will be a tree,"
said Big Nutbrown Hare.

"A big big tree?"

"Oh, a mighty tree,"
said Big Nutbrown
Hare.

Little Nutbrown Hare spotted a tadpole
in a pool. It was a tiny tadpole,
as wriggly as
could be.

"It will grow up to be a frog,"
said Big Nutbrown Hare.

"Like that frog over there?"

"Just the same as that one,"
said Big Nutbrown Hare.

A hairy caterpillar slowly crossed the
path in front of them, in search of
something green to eat.

"One day soon it will change
into a butterfly," said
Big Nutbrown Hare.

"With wings?"

"Oh, lovely wings," said
Big Nutbrown Hare.

And then they found a bird's nest
among the rushes. It was full of eggs.

"What does an egg turn into?" asked
Little Nutbrown Hare.

"A bird."

"A big big bird?"

"Well ... a grown-up bird,"
said Big Nutbrown Hare.

Does nothing stay the same? thought Little Nutbrown Hare. Does everything change?

Then he began to laugh.

"What does a little brown hare like me turn into?" he said.

Big Nutbrown Hare
began to think,

and think...

Goodness me, did he
know the answer?

Yes!

"A Big Nutbrown Hare – like me!"

Summer

Little Nutbrown Hare
and Big Nutbrown Hare were down
by the river on a summer's day.

On a summer's day there
are colours everywhere.

"Which blue do you like best?"
asked Little Nutbrown Hare.

Big Nutbrown Hare didn't know –
there were so many lovely blues.

"I think ... maybe the sky,"
he said.

Big Nutbrown Hare
looked across the river.
There were grasses and ferns
and tall plants swaying
in the breeze.

"Which green do you
like best?" he asked.

Little Nutbrown Hare began to think,
but he didn't really know.
So many lovely things
were green.

"Maybe the big leaves," he said.

Now it was
   Little Nutbrown
   Hare's turn to
   pick a colour.

He spotted a ladybird, and some poppies.

"What's your favourite
red?" he asked.

Big Nutbrown Hare
thought about red things,
but it was hard to choose
just one.

"I think those
berries," he said.

Big Nutbrown Hare nibbled
a dandelion leaf.

"Which yellow do you
like best?"

There were so many yellows!
Little Nutbrown Hare even
saw some yellows
buzzing about.
How could he
possibly choose?

"Maybe these flowers,"
he said.

Then Little Nutbrown Hare began
to smile and smile.

He looked at Big Nutbrown Hare and said,

"Which brown do you like best?"

And Big Nutbrown Hare smiled too.
There were many many lovely browns,
but one was the best of all...

"Nutbrown!"

Autumn

L**ittle Nutbrown Hare**
and Big Nutbrown Hare went out
in the autumn wind.

On a windy day
the leaves are blowing.

They chased after falling leaves
until Big Nutbrown Hare
could chase no more.

"I have to have a rest!" he said.

Then a big brown box came rolling
by, blown by the autumn wind.
Little Nutbrown Hare caught
up with the box when it got
stuck in a bush.

What a fine big box!
It was great for
jumping over ...

jumping on ...

and jumping in.

Big Nutbrown Hare was resting
under a tree when a box
appeared in front of him.
A big brown box.
It gave one hop and then
stood absolutely still.

"I'm a box monster!"
shouted the box.

Goodness me!
Big Nutbrown Hare
blinked his eyes and
wondered if he was
dreaming, for he had
never heard of a box
monster before.

The box, or the monster –
or maybe the box monster –
took two hops forward.

"Here I come!" roared the box,
hopping its biggest hop yet,
and Big Nutbrown Hare
jumped behind the tree.

"I wonder should I run away!" said Big Nutbrown Hare.

"No!" shouted the box, which suddenly flew into the air. "It's only me!"

And there was Little Nutbrown Hare, who could hardly stop laughing.

"You're not a monster,"
said Big Nutbrown Hare.
"But guess what."

"What?"

"I'm a big nutbrown monster –
and I'm coming to
get you!"

And so he did.

Winter

Little Nutbrown Hare
and Big Nutbrown Hare went
out in the winter snow.

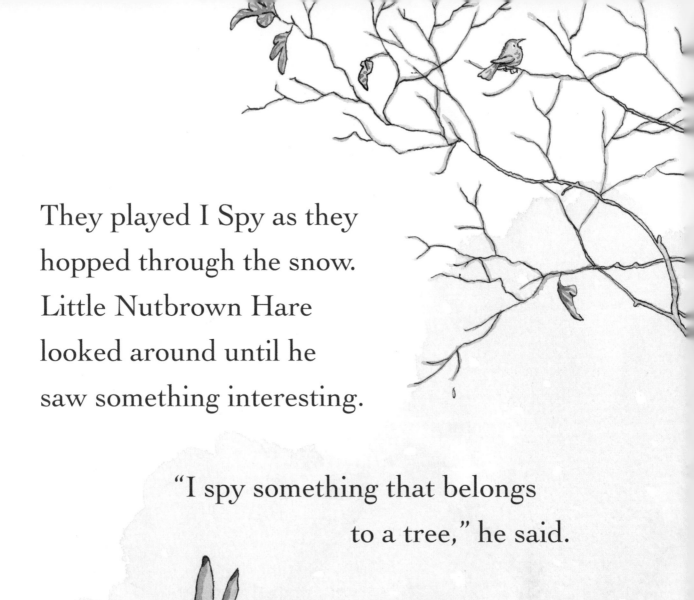

They played I Spy as they
hopped through the snow.
Little Nutbrown Hare
looked around until he
saw something interesting.

"I spy something that belongs
to a tree," he said.

Big Nutbrown Hare
did some thinking
about trees.

"Could it be a leaf?"

It was the right answer!

Now it was Big Nutbrown
Hare's turn to look around him.

"I spy something that
belongs to a spider."

"A web!" said
Little Nutbrown Hare.

Yes! A web was the answer.

"I spy something that
belongs to a bird," said
Little Nutbrown
Hare.

Big Nutbrown
Hare thought
about birds
for a while.

Then he said, "Could it be a feather?"

Yes! It was a feather.

"This time," said
Big Nutbrown Hare, "I spy something that
belongs to the river. And it's wet, wet, wet."

"Water!" cried Little Nutbrown Hare.

Water was the answer.

Little Nutbrown Hare began to laugh.
I've got a good one, he thought.
"I spy something that belongs to me."

Big Nutbrown Hare was puzzled.
"Can I have a clue?" he said.

"It's only there when the
sun comes out."

"Your shadow!" said
Big Nutbrown
Hare.

Then Big Nutbrown Hare said,

"I spy something that belongs to *me*
and it's not my shadow."

This was a really tricky one.
Little Nutbrown Hare did some
thinking, and then he said,

"Can I have a clue?"

"It's little... It's nutbrown...
It's my most favourite thing...

And it can hop."

"Me!"